Workbook

SECOND EDITION

Ken Beatty

HEINLE
CENGAGE Learning™

Australia • Brazil • Japan • Korea • Mexico • Singapore • Spain • United Kingdom • United States

HEINLE
CENGAGE Learning

Go for it! Workbook 1, Second Edition
Ken Beatty

Publisher, Global ELT: Christopher Wenger

Editorial Manager: Berta de Llano

Development Editors: Margarita Matte

Director of Marketing, ESL/ELT: Amy Mabley

International Marketing Manager: Eric Bredenberg

Senior Production Editor: Sally Cogliano

Sr. Print Buyer: Mary Beth Hennebury

Project Manager: Kris Swanson

Interior Design/Composition: Miguel Angel Contreras Pérez; Israel Muñoz Olmos

Illustrators: Iñaki (Ignacio Ochoa Bilbao), Jaime Rivera Contreras

Photo Manager: Sheri Blaney

Photo Researcher: Jill Engebretson

Cover Designer: Linda Beaupre

Photo Credits: 4: all © Heinle; 7: B: © Hemera Photo Objects; 13: TL: © Anders Ryman/CORBIS; TR: © Jack Hollingsworth/CORBIS; B: © Heinle; 22: both: © Heinle; 23: © Reuters NewMedia Inc./CORBIS; 24: Heinle; 26: © Heinle; 28: © Heinle; 29: © Heinle; 31: © Heinle; 35: TL: © UPI/Landov; TLC: © Stock Montage/Index Stock Imagery; TR: © Paul Katz/Index Stock Imagery; T, 2nd from R: Public Domain; BL: © AP Photo/The Charlotte Observer, Gary O'Brien; BR: © Index Stock Imagery; 42: TR: Don Romero/Index Stock Imagery; rest: © Heinle; 46: all: © Heinle; 47: all: © Heinle; 48: © Heinle; 51: both: © Heinle; 55: © Heinle; 60: TL: PhotoDisc Green/Getty Images; BR: Lawrence Ruggeri/Index Stock Imagery; rest: © Heinle; 74: TL: Ralph Reinhold/Index Stock Imagery; TC: Gary Vestal/Index Stock Imagery; TR: Joe Lange/Index Stock Imagery; ML: Zefa Visual Media/Index Stock Imagery; BL: Mark Miller/Index Stock Imagery; BR: Lynn Stone/Index Stock Imagery

For product information and technology assistance, contact us at
Cengage Learning Customer & Sales Support, 1-800-354-9706

For permission to use material from this text or product,
submit all requests online at **www.cengage.com/permissions**
Further permissions questions can be emailed to
permissionrequest@cengage.com

ISBN-13: 978-1-4130-0016-0

ISBN-10: 1-4130-0016-9

Heinle
20 Channel Center Street
Boston, MA 02210
USA

Cengage Learning is a leading provider of customized learning solutions with office locations around the globe, including Singapore, the United Kingdom, Australia, Mexico, Brazil, and Japan. Locate your local office at **www.cengage.com/global**

Cengage Learning products are represented in Canada by Nelson Education, Ltd.

Visit Heinle online at **elt.heinle.com**

Visit our corporate website at **www.cengage.com**

Printed in the United States of America
Print Number: 12   Print Year: 2018

Table of Contents

Unit 1 LESSON A
My name's Gina.

1 **Make questions or sentences with these words.**

1. your   What's   name   first   ?

   <u>What's your first name?</u>

2. is   Anna   name   Her   .

   _____

3. are   names   their   What   ?

   _____

4. George   Their   and   are   Juan   names   .

   _____

5. you   to   meet   Nice   .

   _____

2 **Complete the speech bubbles to make conversations.**

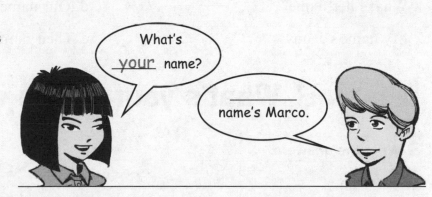

What's <u>your</u> name?

_____ name's Marco.

What's _____ name?

_____ name's Sandra.

What's _____ name?

_____ name's John.

3 Check ✓ the sentences that are correct. Put an ✗ next to the sentences that are incorrect. Rewrite the sentences that are incorrect.

1. I is Marco.   ✗   I am Marco.

2. I'm Alex.   _____   _____

3. Nice to meet me.   _____   _____

4. My name's Mei.   _____   _____

5. I name's Alice.   _____   _____

4 Match the sentences.

1. What's your name?   a. Nice to meet you.

2. What are your names?   b. My name's Roy.

3. What are their names?   c. Her name's Ruth.

4. What's her name?   d. Our names are Bob and Pat.

5. My name's Jenny.   e. Their names are Alison and Carol.

LESSON B What's your phone number?

5 Write the answers.

1. Six + one   = _____ seven _____

2. Four - two   = _____

3. Ten - five   = _____

4. Eight + two = _____

5. Seven - three = _____

6. Nine - six   = _____

7. Ten - four   = _____

8. One + eight = _____

9. Six + two   = _____

10. Five - four = _____

1 = one	4 = four	7 = seven
2 = two	5 = five	8 = eight
3 = three	6 = six	9 = nine

6 Write the questions.

1. _What's his name?_ His name is Peter.
2. _____ My phone number is 555-9988.
3. _____ My last name is Perez.
4. _____ My first name is Marco.
5. _____ Her name is Alice.

7 Circle the correct word.

1. Maria's phone ((number) / numbers) is 555-0104.
2. What's your phone (name / number), Gordon?
3. Carlos is my (friend / phone).
4. Her (last / first) name's Mary.
5. (Their / My) names are James and Joanne.

8 Read and fill in the chart.

My name's Ken Mishima. My phone number is 555-9862.

My first name's Alice. My last name is Johnson. My phone number is 555-2327.

My name's Alessandra Palos. My phone number is 555-0778.

TELEPHONE LIST		
First Name	Last Name	Telephone Number
Ken		

9 Write about yourself. Use these words: first name, last name, telephone number.

_My _____

_____

_____

Greetings

Look at the pictures and read the different ways to say hello.

Now, write the correct greeting for these people.

Unit 2

Is that your ruler?

1 What's that? That's ...

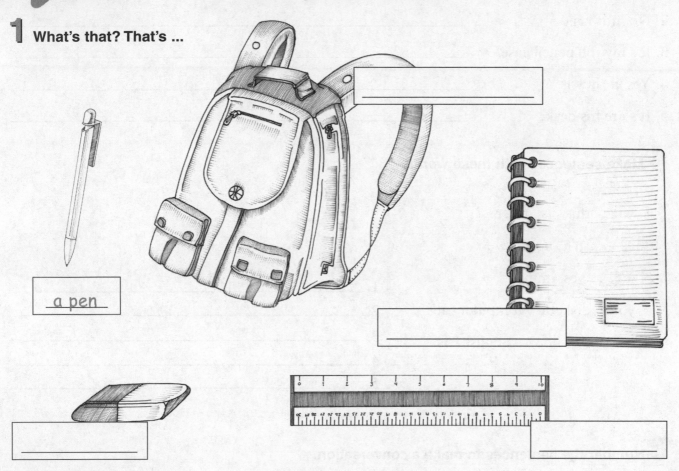

a pen

2 Use the alphabet code to read and then write the message.

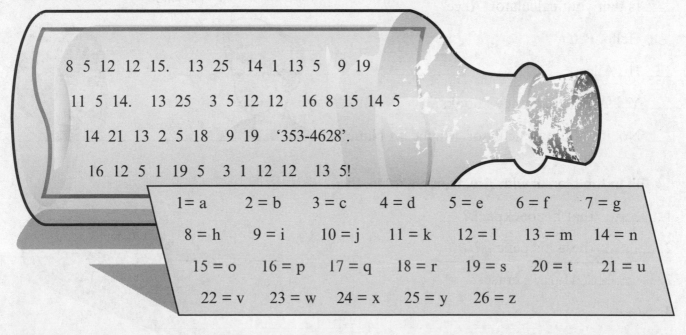

8 5 12 12 15.   13 25   14 1 13 5   9 19

11 5 14.   13 25   3 5 12 12   16 8 15 14 5

14 21 13 2 5 18   9 19   '353-4628'.

16 12 5 1 19 5   3 1 12 12   13 5!

1= a	2 = b	3 = c	4 = d	5 = e	6 = f	7 = g
8 = h	9 = i	10 = j	11 = k	12 = l	13 = m	14 = n
15 = o	16 = p	17 = q	18 = r	19 = s	20 = t	21 = u
22 = v	23 = w	24 = x	25 = y	26 = z		

Message: _____

3 Cross out the word that does not belong in each sentence. Rewrite the sentence.

1. Is this your he calculator? _____

2. No, it it isn't. _____

3. It's my the pencil case. _____

4. Yes, it they is. _____

5. It's are his desk. _____

4 Make sentences with these words.

1. your   this   is   ruler   ?

2. it   ,   isn't   no   .

3. it's   ,   yes   mine   .

4. your   diskette   computer   it's   .

5. her   this   book   English   is   ?

1. Is this your ruler? _____

2. _____

3. _____

4. _____

5. _____

5 Number the sentences to make a conversation.

____ No, they aren't. They're mine.

____ Is that your calculator, Alice?

____ Hello, Peter.

_1_ Hi, Alice.

____ Yes. Are these Nancy's books?

____ No, it's not my calculator. Maybe it's Nancy's.

Hi, Alice.

6 Fill in the blanks with Are, Is, isn't, mine, this.

1. _____ that his backpack?

2. _____ these his pencils?

3. Is _____ Harry's eraser?

4. No, it _____ .

5. This backpack is _____ .

LESSON B Lost and found

7 Rewrite each sentence using contractions.

1. They are his friends.   They're his friends.
2. It is not his backpack.   _____
3. They are not Ellen's computer disks.   _____
4. It is my eraser.   _____
5. We are Sally's teachers.   _____

8 Unscramble the letters to make words.

1. leltaw   wallet   2. areser _____   3. luctarolac_____

4. tooobkne_____   5. akcapbkc_____

Go for it!
English class

Use the words you know to complete these classroom directions.

Open your _____ to page twenty-five.   A: What's this?   B: It's a _____.

Write your name in your _____.   **Circle** the answer in _____.

8   MY THINGS

9 **Read carefully and circle Andrea's locker.**

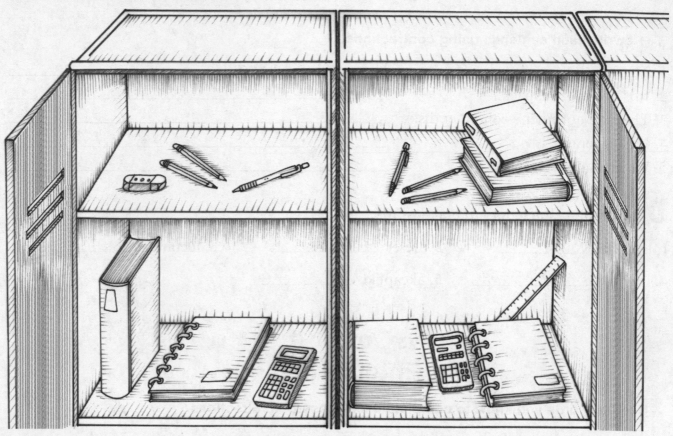

Hi, my name is Andrea. This is my locker. I have many things in my locker. This is my pen and these are my pencils. These are my school books. This is my notebook. This is my calculator and my ruler.

10 **Now write about what you have in your backpack.**

1 Label the people with family words from the box.

mother
father
grandmother
grandfather
sister
brothers

Me

2 Write the words in the correct order.

A: Is your this uncle ?　　　A: <u>Is this your uncle?</u>

B: No, isn't it .　　　B: _____

　my is This father .　　_____

A: your sisters these Are ?　A: _____

B: aren't they No, .　　　B: _____

　cousins These are my .　_____

3 (Circle) the correct word in each response.

1. Are they your cousins?　　　No, they're my (friends / sister).

2. Is this your mother?　　　　No, this (is / are) my aunt.

3. Is that your friend?　　　　No. She's my (brother / sister).

4. Are those your grandparents?　No. (This / These) are my parents.

5. These are my grandparents.　(They / She) are Sue and Jeremy.

6. This is my uncle.　　　　　(He's / She's) Michael.

4 Find 10 names that identify people. Then write the words on the correct list.

```
P A R E N T S O B A G C X O
T V H E K B G Q D T R O R M
F N C Z H H C O Y K A N A O
I F E U M A O B E R N R W T
Z R F R R T U L E R D I D H
S I S T E R S H M E M N Q E
A E N E F P I V I H O S S R
P N T O R A N T X T T B B I
S D B D F S P N E A H T M L
W G R A N D F A T H E R J J
L Z N I U E N U S R R F S J
C A B R O T H E R S G A S J
R H W L Z I F A T H E R N D
G R A N D P A R E N T S D N
```

Male ♂

_____

_____

_____

Female ♀

_____

_____

_____

_____

Male or female

parents _____

_____

_____

_____

5 Fill in the blanks with the words from the box.

cousins
brothers
grandmother
sisters
cousin

1. Natalie and Rose are _sisters_.

2. Our fathers are _____.

3. Their brother is my _____.

4. Their grandmother is my _____.

5. They are my _____.

LESSON B This is my family.

6 Match the questions and answers.

1. Are these your cousins?

2. Is this your mother?

3. Are you his uncle John?

4. Is this your father?

5. Are you Angela's parents?

a. No, he's my uncle.

b. No, this is my aunt.

c. Yes, they're twins.

d. Yes, we are.

e. Yes. Nice to meet you.

7 Complete the sentences with He, She, They.

This is Emily. This is her family. These are Emily's parents.

_____ are Steve and Mayra. This is her brother.
     1

_____'s Paul. She has two uncles. _____'re
   2   3

twins. That's her grandmother with her uncles, Michael

and Bruce. _____'s Rosie.
               4

8 Now answer the questions in complete sentences for each speaker below.

1. What's your sister's name?

   Paul: _My sister's name is Emily._____

2. What's your brother's name?

   Michael: _____

3. What's your mother's name?

   Bruce: _____

4. What's your mom's name?

   Emily: _____

5. What are your parent's names?

   Paul: _____

Go for it!
Families around the world

Read about three families.

Hi, my name is Wayan. I live in Bali. I have three brothers and two sisters. I live with my mother and father and four uncles and two aunts. My grandmother and grandfather live with us too.

Hello. My name is Chan. I live in Singapore with my mother and father. I have one brother and one sister. Their names are Li and Mei. My grandmother lives with us too.

Pleased to meet you! My name is Madeline. I live in England. I live with my mother and father. I have one brother. His name is George.

Fill in the chart. Add your family information.

	Wayan	Madeline	Chan	Your family
parents	2			
brother				
sister				
uncle				
aunt				
grandmother				
grandfather				

Unit 4 LESSON A
Where's my backpack?

1 **Circle the correct word.**

1. Where (is / are) your book?

2. They (is / are) on the game console.

3. (Is / Are) they under the sofa?

4. No. They (is / are) not.

5. (Are / Is) the book on the chair?

2 **Where are the balls? Complete the sentences with** in, on, under.

1. The ball is _____ the desk.

2. The ball is _____ the desk.

3. The ball is _____ the desk.

3 **Number the sentences to make a conversation.**

____ Where is my backpack?

____ They're in your backpack.

_1_ Where are my pen and pencil?

____ It's under the chair.

____ Where is the chair?

14 AT HOME

4 Unscramble the words.

1. oebkcsoa   <u>bookcase</u>
2. neetliisvo   _____
3. gliinv omor   _____
4. nhtcike   _____
5. omordeb   _____

5 Unscramble the sentences.

1. know don't I .   <u>I don't know.</u> _____
2. keys the the in room Are living ? _____
3. it kitchen Is the in ? _____
4. your Where books are ? _____
5. bed They're my on . _____

6 Look at the picture and write the answers.

1. Is the television in the living room? _____
2. Where are your keys? _____
3. Where are your books? _____
4. Where's my ball? _____
5. Where's my brother's notebook? _____

LESSON B Is my math book on the bed?

7 Look at the picture and correct the sentences.

1. This is my kitchen. <u>This is my living room.</u>

2. The television is in the bookcase. _____

3. The CD case is on the sofa. _____

4. The telephone is on the table. _____

5. The math book is on the bookcase. _____

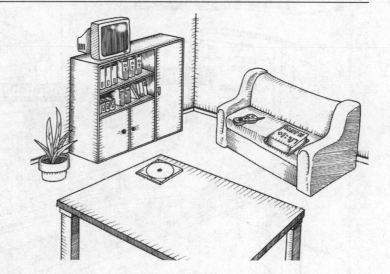

8 Match the questions and answers.

1. Where are my sunglasses?   a. It's on the chair.

2. Where is my CD case?   b. No, they aren't.

3. Is the videocassette in your living room?   c. They're on the sofa.

4. Are your pencils in your backpack?   d. No, my keys are under the sofa.

5. Are your keys on the sofa?   e. No, it isn't. It's in the kitchen.

9 Read the note and fill in the blanks in the chart.

Dear Sally,
Please take these things to your brother:
his math book, ruler, notebook, CDs and
video. The math book is on the dresser.
The ruler is under the bed. The notebook
is on the bed. The CDs are under the
bookcase and the video is on the table.
Thanks, Mom

on	under
math book	

In the science lab

a microscope

a graph

cotton balls

a box

a magnifying glass

a seedling

a binder

a plastic cup

Look at the picture. Complete the sentences with in, on, and under.

1. The binder is _____ the table.

2. The ruler is _____ the binder.

3. The microscope is _____ the shelf.

4. The cotton balls are _____ the box.

5. The seedling is _____ the plastic cup.

Look at the picture again, and write about the location of other objects in the lab.

_____

_____

_____

_____

Review 1

1 Write the missing words in the blanks and in the crossword.

Down

2. My aunt's child is my _____.
3. My bed is in my _____.
5. My father's _____ is my grandmother.
7. _____ is my backpack?
9. Hello, I'm _____ to meet you.
10. The television is in the living _____.
11. _____ name is Mary.

Across

1. My _____ is in my pencil case.
4. What's your first _____?
6. My cousin's father is my _____.
8. _____ names are George and Juan.

Crossword grid with 1 Across: p e n c i l

2 Write these words in alphabetical order.

baseball   1. _____
welcome   2. _____
uncle   3. _____
videocassette   4. _____
keys   5. _____
television   6. _____
calculator   7. _____
eraser   8. _____
grandfather   9. _____

3 (Circle) the correct word.

1. Hi, Kelly, are my keys (in / under) the kitchen?
2. Is your sister (on / in) your bedroom?
3. Is your book (on / in) the chair?
4. Where (is / isn't) the game console?
5. Uncle, is your (kitchen / television) in the living room?

4 Read the scrambled telephone conversation. Write the sentences in the correct order.

Are my sunglasses and math book in your class?

Hello, Mr Black.

Hi, Liz.

I'm your new student.

My name is Liz Reese.

See you in class.

Thanks.

The math book is on the bookcase.

But your sunglasses aren't in the classroom.

Liz: _____

_____

_____

Mr. Black: _____

_____

Liz: _____

_____

Mr. Black: _____

_____

_____

Liz: _____

_____

Mr. Black: _____

_____

To: Mr Black.
From: Liz Reese
Phone number: 555-8979
Message:

5 Fill in the missing letters to spell a new word.

		w	h	e	r	e
	s	_	v	e	n	
	h	e	_	l	o	
p	e	n	_	i	l	
	p	h	_	n	e	
		_	o	t	h	e	r
	k	_	y	s		

6 Number the sentences to make a conversation.

____ It's on a table in the classroom.

____ Nice to meet you, Peter. I'm Nancy.

_1_ Hi, What's your name?

____ Where is your math book, Nancy?

____ My name's Peter. Welcome to our class.

Hi, What's your name?

Unit 5 LESSON A
Do you have a baseball?

1 **Fill in the missing letters to label the pictures.**

1. ___ ___nn___ ___ r___ ___k___t

2. s___ ___ ___ ___ ___ r b___ ___ ___ ___

3. v___ ___ ___ ___ ___ y ___ ___ ___ ___ ___l

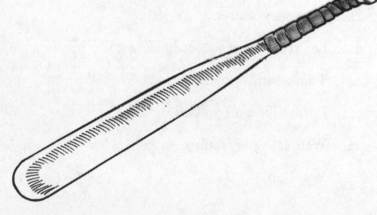

4. ___ ___ ___k___ ___ ___ ___ ___ll

5. b___ ___ ___ ___ ___ ___ ___ ___l b___ ___ ___

2 **Match the questions and sentences to a response.**

1. Do you have a computer game?   a. Hmm. Let's ask.

2. Does he have rollerblades?   b. I think I have two tennis balls, too.

3. Let's play hockey!   c. Let's play soccer.

4. I have two tennis balls.   d. No, I don't.

5. I have a soccer ball.   e. That sounds good.

3 Write the answers.

1. Do you have a TV?   <u>No, I don't.</u>
2. Does she have rollerblades?   Yes, _____
3. Does he have a tennis ball?   No, _____
4. Do they have a basketball?   Yes, _____
5. Do you have a computer game? Yes, _____

4 Complete the sentences with has or have.

1. Does your brother _____ rollerblades?

2. Mary _____ a baseball bat.

3. Yuko and Akira _____ a computer.

4. Do they _____ two tennis rackets?

5. My sister _____ a soccer ball.

5 Number the sentences to make a conversation.

<u>1</u> Let's play baseball.

____ I don't have a tennis racket.

____ Let's play soccer.

____ Do you have a soccer ball?

____ That sounds good.

____ I don't have a baseball.

____ Well, let's play tennis.

____ Yes, I do.

Let's play baseball.

6 Answer the questions with information that is true for you.

1. Do you play soccer? _____

2. Does your friend have a baseball bat? _____

3. Do you play tennis? _____

4. Does your friend have rollerblades? _____

5. Do you have a basket ball? _____

LESSON B **Computer games are fun.**

7 Unscramble the words.

1. ufn   <u>fun</u>
2. rignob   _____
3. rtiengstnie   _____
4. geitcixn   _____
5. rtega   _____
6. lcftdifiu   _____

8 Now write the words in the correct column.

      😃   ☹️

<u>fun</u> _____   _____

_____   _____

_____   _____

9 Read about the sports at two schools. Write the names of the sports in the correct places on the diagram.

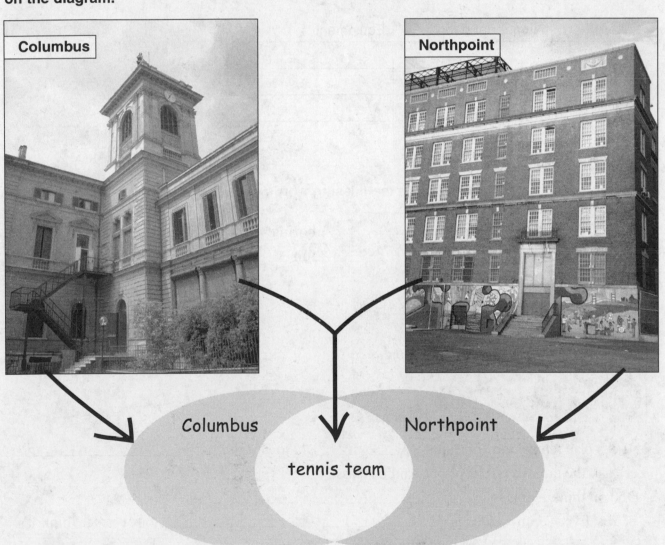

Columbus

Northpoint

tennis team

Columbus School has a tennis team. It also has a baseball team, a soccer team and a basketball team. Northpoint School has a volleyball team. It also has a soccer team, a baseball team and a tennis team.

Read about teams and fill in the chart.

Make a team

Do you have a brother or a sister? Do you have two tennis rackets and a tennis ball? You can play tennis. Two people or four people can play tennis. Do you have a basketball? Do you have two brothers or sisters and can your mother and father play? You have a team for basketball. Volleyball needs six people for each team and a volley ball. But baseball needs a big family. A baseball team has nine people. You need a baseball bat and a ball.

	Number of people	Equipment
baseball		
tennis	two or four	
basketball		
volleyball		

Read about Andre Agassi and fill in the missing words.

boring	difficult	exciting
fun	interesting	great

Let's play tennis! Do you think it's _____? Do you think it's _____?
Let's ask the famous tennis player Andre Agassi.
"Do you think tennis is _____?"
   "Yes. Every tennis game is _____, but I never think it's
_____. I play tennis everyday!"

Sometimes two people play tennis. Sometimes four people play. Do you have a tennis ball and two tennis rackets? You can play tennis too!

Unit 6

LESSON A
Do you like bananas?

1 Label the foods.

sushi
salad
bananas
oranges
sandwich

2 Match the questions and answers.

1. Do you like french fries?
2. Docs she like bananas?
3. Does he like oranges?
4. Do they like tomatoes?
5. What do you like to eat?

a. I like hamburgers.
b. No, he doesn't.
c. Yes, she does.
d. Yes, I do.
e. No, they don't.

3 Fill in the blanks with words from the box.

love   like   likes   don't   doesn't

Sandy: What do you like to eat, Mike?

Mike: Well, I __like__ salad, but
      I _____ like broccoli.

Sandy: And your friend? What does he
      like to eat?

Mike: He _____ oranges and bananas.
      He _____ like hamburgers.

Bob: And I really _____ ice cream.

4 Check ✓ the questions that are correct. Put an ✗ next to the questions that are incorrect and rewrite them.

1. Does you like sushi?   ✗   Do you like sushi?
2. Does he likes salad?   _____   _____
3. Do they likes hamburger?   _____   _____
4. Does she like french fries?   _____   _____
5. Do you like eggs?   _____   _____

5 Find ten food words in the puzzle. Then write the words on the correct list.

```
D  C  A  R  R  O  T  S  E  W  S  G  A  S  E
S  B  A  S  E  N  S  A  L  A  D  G  C  X  G
H  A  V  A  E  S  U  S  H  I  Q  D  T  H  G
S  N  N  Z  H  H  C  O  Y  T  A  U  A  S
K  A  F  D  U  B  R  O  C  C  O  L  I  M  T
E  N  R  W  R  R  T  R  L  E  M  D  I  B  H
S  A  I  I  T  E  R  A  H  M  A  M  N  U  E
K  S  U  C  H  I  P  N  V  I  T  O  S  R  R
O  P  N  H  O  R  A  G  T  X  O  T  B  G  I
G  S  D  E  D  F  S  E  N  E  E  H  T  E  L
B  W  G  S  A  N  D  S  A  T  S  E  R  R  J
S  L  Z  N  I  U  E  N  U  S  R  R  F  S  J
```

Fruits	Vegetables	Other foods
_____	_____	_____
_____	_____	_____
_____	_____	_____
_____	_____	_____

6 Write sentences with these words.

1. like you cream ice Do ?   Do you like ice cream?
2. don't cream like chocolate ice We .   _____
3. like I oranges don't .   _____
4. salad love I !   _____
5. fries I like french really .   _____

LESSON B I like some fruit, but I hate bananas.

7 Write the foods Anna loves and hates. Then write the foods you love and hate.

Anna loves…   Anna hates…   I love…   I hate…

<u>broccoli</u>

_____   _____   _____   _____

_____   _____   _____   _____

_____   _____   _____   _____

_____   _____   _____   _____

8 Read an article about healthy and unhealthy foods.

Be healthy!

Do you eat healthy food for breakfast, lunch and dinner? It's important. Oranges, watermelon and apples are healthy, but too much ice cream is unhealthy. I love carrots and string beans. They are healthy, but french fries are not healthy.

Now, answer the questions.

1. Is watermelon healthy?   <u>Yes, it is.</u> _____

2. Are french fries unhealthy?   _____

3. Are carrots healthy?   _____

4. Are string beans unhealthy?   _____

5. Are oranges and apples healthy? _____

9 What do you eat for breakfast, lunch and dinner?

<u>At breakfast, I eat…</u> _____

_____

_____

Go for it!
A healthy diet

Write the names of the foods in the correct column on the chart.

carrots	broccoli	string beans	apples	eggs

donut	yogurt	beef steak	roast chicken	rice

Dairy	Meat and Fish	Bread and Cereal	Fruit and Vegetables

Can you add more foods to the chart?

Unit 7

1 **Cross out the word that does not belong in each sentence.**

1. How much are ~~this~~ these sneakers?
2. The bags is cost nine dollars.
3. Let's blue buy a pair of shorts.
4. Harry likes like the sweatshirt.
5. It's costs four dollars.

2 **Match the sentences.**

1. How much does this wallet cost?
2. How much are these sneakers?
3. I like the blue bag!
4. I like the yellow pair of shorts.
5. How much is it?

a. They're ten dollars.
b. It's five dollars.
c. I like the green pair.
d. I don't. I like the red one.
e. The wallets cost eight dollars.

3 **Use the picture to write sentences with This is my… or These are my…**

1. This is my sweater.
2. _____
3. _____
4. _____
5. _____

4 Check ✔ the questions that are correct. Put an ✗ next to the questions that are not correct. Then rewrite the questions.

1. Can I helps you?   ✗   Can I help you?

2. How much is this sweater?   ____   _____

3. How much are that pants?   ____   _____

4. How much is these bag?   ____   _____

5. How much are these socks?   ____   _____

5 Number the sentences to make a conversation.

_1_ How much is this hat?

____ I'll take it.

____ It's nine dollars.

____ You're welcome.

____ Thank you.

____ Here's your hat.

6 Find 5 colors and 5 clothing words in the puzzle. Write the words below.

```
G  S  D  B  D  F  S  P  N  E  A  H  T  M  L
A  X  A (R  E  D) T  T  O  B  A  G  C  X  O
H  T  V  H  E  K  B  S  Q  S  H  O  R  T  S
S  B  E  I  G  E  H  H  O  Y  K  A  Y  A  O
K  L  F  E  U  M  B  I  A  C  K  N  E  W  Z
E  A  R  F  R  R  T  R  L  E  R  D  L  D  H
S  W  I  M  S  U  I  T  H  M  E  B  L  U  E
K  K  E  S  N  E  A  K  E  R  S  V  O  H  O
O  P  N  T  O  R  A  N  T  X  T  T  W  B  I
B  L  A  C  K  N  D  H  A  Z  H  E  T  J  J
```

Colors
_____
_____
_____
_____
_____

Clothes
_____
_____
_____
_____
_____

LESSON B The shorts are sixteen dollars.

7 Unscramble the letters and write the numbers after the correct equation.

efeotunr   1. twenty-three + eight = _____

neo neddurh   2. seventy + thirty   = _____

nttywe-sxi   3. seven + nineteen   = _____

neeelv   4. twenty-nine - fifteen = _____

yhritt-noe   5. ninety - seventy-nine= _____

8 Read about Henry and write the prices on the price tags.

    Henry is shopping. Henry buys socks. They cost three dollars. He buys a cap. It costs ten dollars. He buys a pair of shorts. They cost fourteen dollars. He buys a T-shirt. It costs nine dollars. He buys a sweater. It's seventeen dollars. Henry buys blue jeans. They cost twenty-three dollars. He buys sneakers. They cost forty-three dollars.

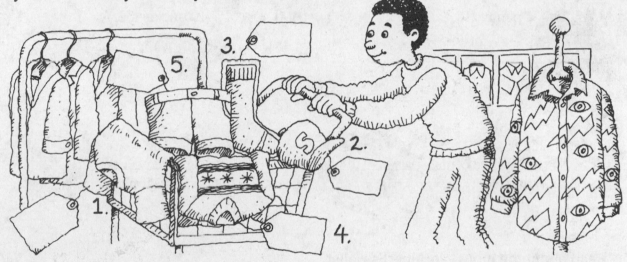

9 Write a paragraph about what Sarah buys. Use words (seven), not numbers (7).

Sarah is shopping. She buys...

_____

_____

_____

_____

_____

_____

_____

_____

Go for it!
American money

dollar: $1, one dollar, a dollar bill

penny: 1¢,
one cent,
a penny

nickel: 5¢,
five cents,
a nickel

quarter: 25¢,
twenty-five cents,
a quarter

dime: 10¢,
ten cents,
a dime

Read about the money in Albert's wallet.

It's really hot today. I need a new sun hat. The sun hat costs four dollars. Do I have enough money in my wallet? Let's see. I have three pennies. That's three cents. I have two nickels. Each nickel is five cents. I have three dimes. That's thirty cents. I only have one quarter. That's twenty-five cents. And I have three dollar bills. That's three dollars. How much is that?

Now, answer these questions.

1. How much money does Albert have in his wallet? _____
2. Can he buy the hat? _____
3. How much is two dimes and a nickel? _____
4. How much is four quarters? _____
5. How much is five pennies? _____
6. How much is ten cents and three nickels? _____
7. How much is ten dimes? _____

Unit 8

LESSON A
My birthday's on November 11th.

1 **Circle the months of the year, and then write them in order.**

```
S   P   M   A   Y   N   T   S   O   B   A   S   C   X   O
H   T   V   U   E   K   J   G   Q   D   T   E   O   R   M
F   F   N   G   Z   M   A   R   C   H   K   P   D   A   O
E   I   F   U   U   M   N   O   B   E   R   T   E   W   T
B   Z   R   S   R   J   U   N   E   E   R   E   C   D   H
R   S   I   T   T   E   A   P   R   I   L   M   E   Q   E
U   A   E   N   E   F   R   I   V   I   H   B   M   S   R
A   A   R   J   U   L   Y   N   T   X   T   E   B   B   I
R   S   D   B   D   O   C   T   O   B   E   R   E   M   L
Y   W   N   O   V   E   M   B   E   R   H   E   R   J   J
```

January		
___1 2 3___	___1 2 3 4 5 6 7___	___1 2 3 4 5 6___
4 5 6 7 8 9 10	8 9 10 11 12 13 14	7 8 9 10 11 12 13
11 12 13 14 15 16 17	15 16 17 18 19 20 21	14 15 16 17 18 19 20
18 19 20 21 22 23 24	22 23 24 25 26 27 28	21 22 23 24 25 26 27
25 26 27 28 29 30 31	29	28 29 30 31

___1 2 3___	___1___	___1 2 3 4 5___
4 5 6 7 8 9 10	2 3 4 5 6 7 8	6 7 8 9 10 11 12
11 12 13 14 15 16 17	9 10 11 12 13 14 15	13 14 15 16 17 18 19
18 19 20 21 22 23 24	16 17 18 19 20 21 22	20 21 22 23 24 25 26
25 26 27 28 29 30	23 24 25 26 27 28 29	27 28 29 30
	30 31	

___1 2 3___	___1___	___1 2 3 4 5___
4 5 6 7 8 9 10	2 3 4 5 6 7 8	6 7 8 9 10 11 12
11 12 13 14 15 16 17	9 10 11 12 13 14 15	13 14 15 16 17 18 19
18 19 20 21 22 23 24	16 17 18 19 20 21	20 21 22 23 24 25 26
25 26 27 28 29 30 31	22 23 24 25 26 27 28	27 28 29 30 31
	29 30	

2 **Cross out the word that does not belong in each sentence.**

1. When's your ~~our~~ birthday?
2. Is in your birthday in March?
3. Mine my is on November 10th.
4. My birthday is in January two.
5. When is yours you?

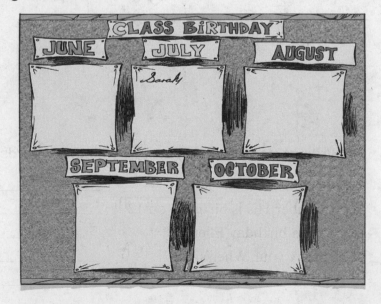

3 Look at the chart and fill in the missing words and numbers.

Ordinal numbers			
1st	first	21st	
2nd	second		thirty-second
3rd		43rd	
4th	fourth	54th	
5th		65th	
6th		76th	
	seventh	87th	
	eighth	98th	
	ninth		ninety-ninth
	tenth	100th	

4 Write sentences and questions with these words.

1. April in is birthday My .   My birthday is in April. _____

2. November His is birthday on 12th . _____

3. is When birthday Ellen's ? _____

4. birthday your When's ? _____

5. February is on Mine 15th . _____

LESSON B When is the class party?

5 **Match the questions and answers.**

1. When is your birthday?
2. When is the English test?
3. When is your brother's birthday?
4. When is the Arts Festival?
5. Is the basketball game on February 5th ?

a. It's on October 20th.
b. No, it's on February 9th .
c. My birthday is in April.
d. It's on November 1st to November 3rd.
e. His birthday is on January 3rd.

6 **Read the paragraph and fill in the calendar.**

April is a busy month! There are English tests on April 9th and April 23rd. Our class play is on April 5th. It's part of The Shakespeare Arts Festival. It's on the 5th and 6th. Thomas Jefferson's birthday is on April 13th. It's not a holiday. We have classes that day. But we have a class trip on April 20th and a basketball game on April 30th.

APRIL

Monday	Tuesday	Wednesday	Thursday	Friday	Saturday	Sunday
			1	2	3	4
5	6	7	8	9 English test	10	11
12	13	14	15	16	17	18
19	20	21	22	23	24	25
26	27	28	29	30		

7 **Do you know people with birthdays in April? Add other April birthdays to the calendar, and write a list of your friends' birthdays.**

_____

_____

_____

_____

_____

Go for it!
Holidays

Fill in the blanks with words from the box.

1st	25th	are	December	fun	holiday	holidays	It's	year

When is your favorite _holiday_ ? Many _____ are in December. _____ 12th is the day when people celebrate the Virgin of Guadalupe in Mexico. December 21st is the shortest day of the _____. _____ called the Winter Solstice. Christmas is on December _____. In America, Kwanzaa is from December 26th to January 1st. New Year's Day is on January _____ in most countries. Other holidays, like Ramadan and Hanukkah _____ on different days each year. It's _____ to have many holidays.

Here are some American Holidays.

Martin Luther King Jr. Day is the third Monday in January.

President's Day is the third Monday in February.

Independence Day is on July 4th.

Labor Day is the first Monday in September.

Thanksgiving is the fourth Thursday in November.

What are the names and dates of the holidays you know?

_____

_____

_____

Review 2

1 Write the missing words in the blanks and in the crossword.

		¹b			²				
	³	a							
		s					⁴		
⁵		e			⁶				
		b							
	⁷	a		⁸					
		l	⁹						
¹⁰		l							

Down

1. You play _____ with a bat and a ball.
2. Hamburgers are good with _____ fries.
4. The last month of the year is _____.
6. It's not exciting, it's _____.
9. . . . April, _____, June . . .

Across

3. The first month of the year is _____.
5. I love to eat ice _____.
7. The swimsuits and sneakers are in my _____.
8. . . . 12 _____ 14 . . .
10. There are one hundred pennies in a _____.

2 Unscramble the sentences.

1. tomatoes do What the cost red ?   _____

2. birthday Is your 13 August on ?   _____

3. dollar french The fries one cost .   _____

4. about and you friend your How ?   _____

5. 20th class Our is party December on .   _____

3 (Circle) the correct word.

1. (Mine / My) is on December 24th, too.
2. Is (you / your) birthday on September 12th?
3. When (is / are) the school play?
4. Do you (like / likes) sushi and ice cream?
5. I like pants, but I (don't / do) like blue jeans.

4 What would you buy with ten dollars? List the items.

_____

_____

_____

_____

_____

_____

5 Fill in the missing letters to spell a new word.

	f	r	i	e	n	d	
	s	_	v	e	n		
		_	a	l	a	d	
p	a	n	_	s			
		b	_	r	t	h	d	a	y
	f	i	e				
	o	r	_	n	g	e	s
A	p	r	i	_			

6 Number the sentences to make a conversation.

_____ Do you like this red bathing suit?

_____ Hello, welcome. Can I help you?

_____ Here you are. And happy birthday!

_1_ Hi.

_____ It's twenty-three dollars.

_____ Mm. Twenty-three dollars. Okay.

_____ No, I don't. How much is the black bathing suit?

_____ Yes. It's my birthday. I want a new bathing suit.

My reading journal

Read Danger on White Water. Complete the journal page.

Title: Danger on White Water

Author:

I think the story is

Important characters:

My favorite character is

I don't like

Setting (where the story happens)

Draw a map or picture of the setting.

Write a dialog of your own.

What happens next?

Write the dialog or draw a picture.

Self check

Do you use English outside your classroom? Check ✓ the boxes.

	often	sometimes	never
I read English newspapers.	☐	☐	☐
I read English magazines.	☐	☐	☐
I read English books.	☐	☐	☐
I listen to English radio or music.	☐	☐	☐
I watch English television or movies.	☐	☐	☐

What's the best thing in English you've read, listened to or watched this week.

_____

Can you do these things?

1 **Write the questions for these answers.**

A: _____? B: His name's Bob.

A: _____? B: No, I'm 15 years old.

A: _____? B: Their phone number is 555-9232.

A: _____? B: No, this is my sister, Ellen.

A: _____? B: Her friend's birthday is in August.

2 **Tick the boxes and write an example.**

☐ ask how words are spelled _____

☐ use and spell numbers _____

☐ ask for prices of different things _____

☐ talk about dates of birthdays and special events _____

☐ talk different foods you like and dislike _____

3 **Write the names of things you have and words that describe them.**

Things I have	Describing words
_____	_____
_____	_____
_____	_____
_____	_____
_____	_____

Unit 9

Do you want to rent a video?

1 **Label the TV screens with the names of different kinds of videos.**

drama _____

_____

_____

_____

_____

_____

2 **Fill in the blanks with words from the box.**

and
do
kinds
but
want
like

A: Do you _____ to rent a movie?

B: Yes, I _____ .

A: What _____ of movies do you _____?

B: I like action movies _____ comedies. What kinds of movies do you like?

A: I like comedies, _____ I don't like action movies.

> What kinds of movies do you like?

_____

3 Circle the correct word.

1. (Does / (Do)) you want to rent a movie?

2. Yes, she (does / do).

3. I (want / wants) to see an action movie.

4. (Want / What) kinds of music videos do you like?

5. Gordon (like / likes) documentaries.

4 Write the questions.

1. Q: _What kinds of movies do you like?_____

   A: I like thrillers, but I don't like romantic movies.

2. Q: _____

   A: No, he doesn't want to rent a movie.

3. Q: _____

   A: No, she doesn't like sports videos.

4. Q: _____

   A: Yes, I want to see a drama.

5. Q: _____

   A: No, we don't want to rent a video.

5 Check ✔ the sentences that are correct. Put an ✕ next to the sentences that are not correct. Then rewrite the sentences.

1. Let's rents two videos.   ✕ _Let's rent two videos._____

2. She doesn't likes romantic movies. ___ _____

3. What kind of movies do you like?   ___ _____

4. I like dramas, thrillers, and documentaries. ___ _____

5. I like music videos but comedies.   ___ _____

LESSON B Thrillers are scary.

6 Draw lines between the opposites.

1. comedy   a. boring
2. fast-moving   b. drama
3. scary   c. funny
4. silly   d. sad
5. spellbinding   e. slow

7 Read about these students' movie preferences.

My name is Elaine. I like romantic movies and thrillers, but I don't like comedies and action movies.

I'm Lee. I like action movies and scary thrillers. I don't like romantic movies.

I'm Patricia. I like comedies, cartoons, and romances. I like thrillers and sci-fi movies, too.

My name is Carlos. I like thrillers, but I don't like comedies. I don't like boring romantic movies.

Answer the questions. Check ✓ T for true and F for false.

	T	F
1. Lee and Patricia both like romantic movies.		
2. Elaine doesn't like action movies.		
3. Carlos thinks romantic movies are spellbinding.		
4. Patricia likes many kinds of movies.		
5. All four like thrillers.		

Go for it!
Book reviews

The name of this adventure is <u>Harry Potter and the Chamber of Secrets</u>. It is an exciting and scary adventure book. It is about magic. A boy and his friends fight many enemies and solve mysteries. It's a movie, too. I like it.

The name of this book is <u>Lord of the Rings</u>. It's a fast-moving thriller. The friends in the story have many adventures. It's a fun book. There is an action movie and a cartoon movie of <u>Lord of the Rings</u>.

The name of this book is <u>Sinbad the Sailor</u>. It's a comedy and an adventure. Sinbad's life is never boring. I like Sinbad and his friends. They're funny.

<u>Cinderella</u> is a silly romantic fairy tale. Cinderella has a mean stepmother and three mean stepsisters. Cinderella usually cleans the house. One day, Cinderella goes to a dance and meets a prince. They fall in love. It's a great story.

Name of the book	Kind of book	Words that describe the book
<u>Lord of the Rings</u>	thriller	fast-moving, fun

Write a review of a book you know.

_____

_____

_____

> **LOOK!**
> When you write the name of the book, underline it. If you are using a computer, write it in *italics*.

Unit 10

Can you play the guitar?

1 **Read and number the pictures. Then, circle the pictures of things you can do.**

1. My friend Wendy is in the chess club.

2. That's Pierre. He can speak English. He can also speak French.

3. Jorge is very funny. He can tell jokes.

4. Ellen is my friend in the art club. She can draw.

5. She's my sister. She can't swim, but she can take photographs.

2 **What can you do? Write answers to these questions**

1. Can you speak English? _Yes, I can._

2. Can you sing? _____

3. Can you dance? _____

4. Can you swim? _____

5. Can you play chess? _____

6. Can you play the guitar? _____

3 Unscramble these words to make questions and answers.

A: play brother the your guitar Can ?
Can your brother play the guitar?

B: can't , he No .

_____

A: play you the Can guitar ?

_____

B: guitar , sing the I play can and Yes .

_____

A: to club music join want Do you our ?

_____

B: do , I yes .

_____

4 Number the sentences to make a conversation.

____ Yes, I can.

____ Do you want to join the Art Club?

____ Can you paint?

_1_ What club do you want to join?

____ Can you swim?

____ No, I can't.

____ Yes, I do.

____ I don't know.

5 Think of two friends. What things can and can't each of them do? Fill in the chart.

My first friend can . . .	My second friend can . . .

Lesson B Bill can play the guitar, but he can't sing.

6 Unscramble the letters to make words.

1. itraug _guitar_
2. mpttrue _____
3. niilov _____
4. opani   _____
5. msudr   _____

7 Now use the words in sentences.

_____
_____
_____
_____
_____

8 Read about four students who want to join the music club. How many things can each do?

Suki
I can't sing, and I can't dance. I can play the violin and the drums.

Angela
I can sing, but I can't dance. I can play the trumpet and the guitar.

Petrus
I can't dance, but I can sing. I can play the violin.

Albert
I can sing and dance. I can play the violin and the drums.

1. Suki can do __2__ things.
2. Angela can do _____ things.
3. Petrus can do _____ things.
4. Albert can do _____ things.
5. Which two students can do the most things? _____ and _____.

9 Start a band. Write what you and your friends can do.

I can . . . _____

_____

_____

Go for it!
Using graphic organizers

Read the paragraph and study the mind map. Circle the things in the mind map that Jeremy can do. Cross out the things that he can't.

There are many clubs and teams at school. I'm on the swim team because I can swim. I want to join the dance club, but I can't dance. There's a choir for people who can sing, but I can't. I speak French, so I belong to the French club. Everyone has to do things in French. I can tell jokes. My friend can act, but I can't. But I can rollerblade, and my friend can't.

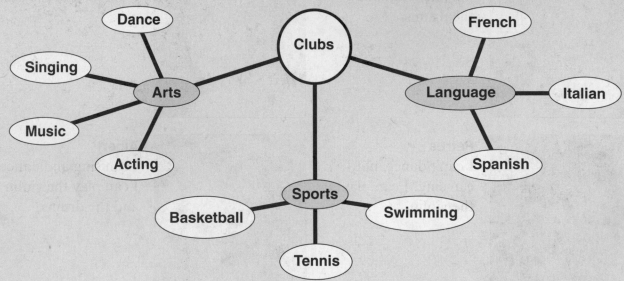

Dance

Singing

Music

Arts

Acting

Clubs

French

Language

Italian

Spanish

Sports

Basketball

Tennis

Swimming

Draw a mind map to show the things you can do.

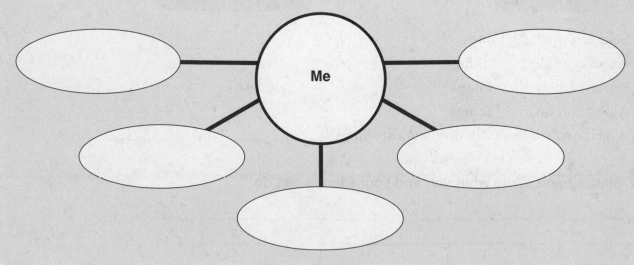

Me

Unit 11 LESSON A
What time do you usually go to school?

1 Unscramble the letters to spell daily routines.

1. tae ktbrafsae   <u>eat breakfast</u>
2. akte a wroehs   _____
3. tge seesddr   _____
4. hurbs hette   _____
5. og to etccirpa   _____

2 Now use the phrases from 1 in sentences that describe your daily routines.

1. _____
2. _____
3. _____
4. _____
5. _____

3 Cross out the word that does not belong. Then rewrite the sentences.

1. When does your dad ~~you~~ usually get up?

_____

2. He usually ~~get~~ gets up at six o'clock.

_____

3. He showers ~~but~~ and eats breakfast before 6:30.

_____

4. Six-thirty? When ~~does~~ do he leave for work?

_____

5. He usually ~~leaves~~ leave at eight o'clock.

_____

4 Match the phrases to make questions.

1. When do you get   a. a shower?
2. What time do you feed   b. breakfast?
3. When do you take   c. your pet?
4. When do you eat   d. for school?
5. What time do you leave   e. dressed?

> ## LOOK!
> We write out times in words at the beginning of a sentence and use numbers in the middle or the end of a sentence:
>
> **Nine o'clock is when the class starts.**
>
> **It finishes at 10:00.**

5 **What does Justin usually do in the morning? Look at the pictures and write a sentence to describe each one.**

_____   _____   _____

_____   _____   _____

6 **Unscramble the sentences.**

1. you leave school for do when usually? <u>When do you usually leave for school?</u>

2. pet time feed what you do your? _____

3. dressed do when get you? _____

4. school to you do what get time? _____

5. do when run for your leave you? _____

7 **Write the questions.**

1. Q: <u>When does she feed her pets?</u> _____

   A: She feeds her pets at 8:00.

2. Q: _____

   A: He usually gets up at 7:45.

3. Q: _____

   A: They leave for school at 8:00.

4. Q: _____

   A: Yes, she usually gets up before 9:00 on weekends.

5. Q: _____

   A: No, I don't usually get to school by 8:30.

LESSON B Healthy living

8 Use the expressions in the box to write sentences about your daily activities. Draw the times on the clocks.

| get up | get dressed | eat breakfast | brush my teeth | leave for school | get to school |

1. I sometimes
get up at 7 o'clock

2. I usually
_____

3. I never
_____

4. I usually
_____

5. I always
_____

6. I never
_____

9 Read about Janet Smith's day and fill in the schedule below.

Janet Smith is a tennis star. She is thirteen years old. She usually gets up at 7:00. She has a shower at seven forty-five and eats breakfast at 8:00. She and her friend play tennis at 8:30. They play tennis for three hours. Janet eats lunch at 12:00. At one fifteen, she plays tennis again. She plays for three hours. At four o'clock, Janet does some exercise, usually a run. At seven-thirty, Janet goes to a karate class. Janet never watches TV. She's too tired!

Time	Activity
7:00 am	gets up
12:00	eats lunch

10 Write about the daily routine of someone you know: your mother, father or friend.

My mother usually gets up at . . .
_____

_____

Go for it!
Daily life around the world

Read about Miguel's and Robert's weeks. Write a list of the things they both do.

Miguel

I usually get up at 7:00 and eat breakfast. I like black beans and rice for breakfast. I usually go to school at 8:00. At 4:00, I go to another school for English lessons. We eat dinner at 7:00 and I usually do my homework at 8:00. Then I like to watch TV or talk to my friends on the telephone. I go to school on Saturday mornings and usually see my friends on Sunday. We like to play soccer. I usually go to bed at 11:00.

Robert

I usually get up at 7:00 and help my mother and father. We have a big sheep ranch. I like eggs for breakfast. There is no school close by. I study at home. I have books, and I listen to classes on the radio. I use my computer, too. I talk to my friends on the telephone. We eat dinner at 6:00. After dinner, I watch T.V. I usually see my friends on Sunday. We like to play tennis and soccer. I read books after dinner or play the guitar. I usually go to bed at ten o'clock.

_____   _____
_____   _____
_____   _____

Write things you do that are the same as Miguel or Robert?

_____
_____
_____

Unit 12 LESSON A
My favorite subject is science.

1 Unscramble the words to make a conversation.

A: you What's subject favorite ? <u>What's your favorite subject?</u>

B: subject My favorite math is . _____

A: math Why like you do ? _____

B: exciting it is Because . _____

A: science you , like too Do ? _____

B: do , yes I . _____

2 Fill in the blanks with the words in the box. Use the cues in brackets.

| his |
| her |
| my |
| your |
| their |

1. What's (you) __your__ favorite subject?
2. Who is (Mary and Alice) _____ math teacher?
3. What are (John) _____ favorite subjects?
4. Why does (Mary) _____ like French?
5. Music is (me) _____ favorite subject.

3 Unscramble the words. Which one is your favorite? Write them in order of most favorite to least favorite.

1. tteeuiarrl _____   _____

2. poeturcm neecics _____   _____

3. aoergghpy _____   _____

4. neesicc _____   _____

5. oirthys _____   _____

4 Match the questions and answers.

1. Why do you hate history?   a. No, I like literature.

2. What's your favorite subject?   b. Because it's boring.

3. Why do your sisters like computer science?   c. Because it's cool.

4. Why does she like her math teacher?   d. My favorite subject's art.

5. Do you like geography?   e. Because she's great.

5 Circle the correct word.

1. ((What) / Who) is your favorite subject?

2. My favorite (subject's / subject) science.

3. Who is your favorite (subject / teacher)?

4. (What / Why) does she hate math?

5. Why (do / does) Eric and Lisa like their math teacher?

Go for it!
School equipment

Write the names of these things under the correct school subject in the chart below. You can write some things more than once.

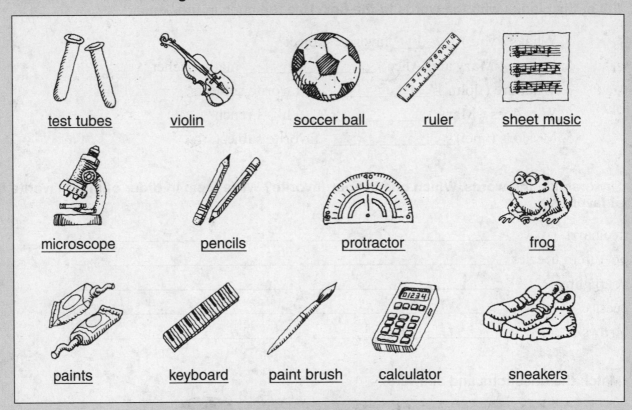

| test tubes | violin | soccer ball | ruler | sheet music |

| microscope | pencils | protractor | | frog |

| paints | keyboard | paint brush | calculator | sneakers |

science	physical education	art	music	math
test tubes				

LESSON B Music is cool.

6 Draw lines to show what you think about different subjects.

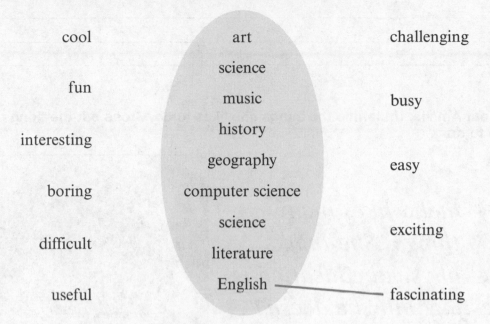

cool

fun

interesting

boring

difficult

useful

art
science
music
history
geography
computer science
science
literature
English

challenging

busy

easy

exciting

fascinating

7 Read the newspaper article and fill in the chart.

Favorite subjects

There are differences between boys' and girls' favorite subjects in school. Many young girls like computer science, math, music and languages. Most young boys think computer science and physical education are cool. Some other subjects are too challenging. But many sixteen year-old boys like science and math. Many sixteen year-old girls think languages like English, Spanish, French and Chinese are fascinating. Although some girls think science and math are great, too. Why do boys and girls have different favorite subjects? We don't know.

Young girls	Young boys	Sixteen year-old girls	Sixteen year-old boys
computer science			

8 Write about your favorite subjects. Mention your books and the special equipment you use as well as your teachers, your favorite activities and why you like them.

My favorite . . . _____

_____

_____

_____

9 Read about Amelia. Underline the things she likes to do. Cross out the things that she doesn't like to do.

Amelia likes many things. She thinks physical education is interesting, but she doesn't like soccer or basketball. She likes tennis. Amelia also likes fine arts. She likes painting, but she doesn't like ceramics. She likes music, too. She likes to sing and play the guitar. Amelia also likes dancing.

10 Write five things you like and don't like to do.

Like to do	Don't like to do

Review 3

1 Complete the crossword.

Down

1.    2.    4.

7. It's not difficult, it's _____.

8. I don't like math, _____ I do like science.

9.

Across

3. He likes to _____ jokes.

5. I can play the _____.

6. I like _____ movies.

8. I get up at 7:00 and eat _____.

(crossword grid)

2 Unscramble the sentences.

1. favorite What club is your?   <u>What is your favorite club?</u>

2. club I the like music.   _____

3. class Is your favorite music?   _____

4. Yes. play guitar the piano I Because the and.   _____

5. want music I join club the to.   _____

3 (Circle) the correct word to complete the conversation:

John: What (when / time) do you usually get up?

Mary: I (get / go) up at 5:00.

John: Wow! (That's / Then) early, isn't it?

Mary: Yes, but I exercise. I (swim / science class) from 5:30 to 7:30.

John: You like keeping (healthy / unhealthy)!

4 Number the things in order by time.

Cineplex 3
Saturday 12 October
11:45 am $8:00

10:05

Math class,
Teacher: Mrs. Sherman,
Rm. 409, 9:20

OCTOBER

12

Saturday

October
S M T W T F S
        1 2 3
4 5 6 7 8 9 10
11 12 13 14 15 16 17
18 19 20 21 22 23 24
25 26 27 28 29 30 31

soccer practice, 2:00 pm

Mary Jane's café
breakfast
7:00 - 8:00

am = in the morning
pm = in the afternoon

5 Fill in the missing letters to spell a new word. Then write sentences using more than one word from the puzzle in each. Try to write as few sentences as possible.

_____

_____

_____

_____

c	o	m	e	d	y		
s	c	i	e	_	c	e	
	e	i	_	h	t		
		_	e	a	v	e	
		v	_	d	e	o	
s	p	o	r	t	_		
	_	i	s	t	o	r	y

6 Number the sentences 1 to 10 to make a conversation.

___ Because the teacher is so interesting.

_1_ Hey, Jean, what time is your karate practice?

___ I go from practice to school, about 8:30.

___ It's at 9:00. It's math class. I love it.

___ That's early!

___ Practice is at 7:00.

___ What time do you leave for school?

___ When is your first class?

___ Why do you love it?

___ Yes, it is. I get up and have a shower at 6:30.

7 Look at the letters in geography. How many other words can you make with these letters?

page,_____

_____

Unit 13

Where is your e-pal from?

1 Label the countries.

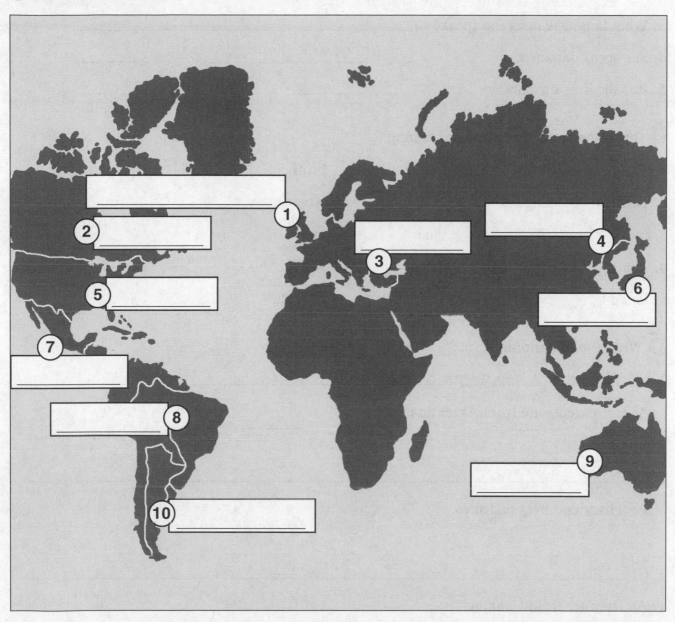

2 Number the sentences to make a conversation.

_1_ Do you have an e-pal?

___ What language does Thomas speak?

___ Where do thcy live?

___ Thomas speaks English and Chinese.

___ Yes, I have two e-pals.

___ Petra lives in Argentina, and Thomas lives in Australia.

3 Check ✔ the sentences that are correct. Put an ✗ next to the sentences that are not correct and rewrite them.

1. Where does they live? ✗ Where do they live?

2. She's from Japanese. ___ _____

3. What language does she speak? ___ _____

4. She speak Japanese. ___ _____

5. But she lives on Turkey. ___ _____

4 Circle the word that does not belong.

1. (language)   sister   mother   brother

2. Turkey   English   USA   Korea

3. speak   city   like   live

4. what   why   from   where

5. Japan   New York   Brazil   Canada

5 Write the questions.

1. Q: Where are her parents from?

   A: Her parents are from Argentina.

2. Q: _____

   A: His friend lives in Tokyo.

3. Q: _____

   A: They are from Canada.

4. Q: _____

   A: Her brother lives in Mexico City.

5. Q: _____

   A: They speak Spanish in Peru.

LESSON B What languages do you speak?

6 Write these words in alphabetical order.

| nationality |
| languages |
| Taiwanese |
| American |
| French |
| Brazilian |
| Argentinean |
| Canadian |
| Chinese |
| Australian |

1. _____
2. _____
3. _____
4. _____
5. _____

6. _____
7. _____
8. _____
9. _____
10. _____

7 Read about four e-pals. Which two people do you want for your e-pals. Why?

Kim
My name is Kim. I'm Korean. I live in Seoul, Korea. I like basketball and baseball. I speak three languages: Korean, Japanese and English. I don't like art or dancing.

Juanita
My name is Juanita. I live in the United States. I like chess and I swim. My favorite subject in school is P.E. I speak Spanish and English. I love music. I like documentaries.

Alessandro
My name is Alessandro. I live in Rio de Janeiro, Brazil. I like baseball and my favorite subject in school is music. I play the guitar and the piano. I like action movies and thrillers.

Ming
My name is Ming. I live in Toronto, Canada and I speak Chinese, French, and English. My favorite subject is art. I play tennis. My favorite movies are comedies and romances. I don't like thrillers.

I want _____ and _____ for my e-pals because _____

_____

8 Write about one of your friends.

Andre lives in the United States, but his
nationality is French. He speaks French
and English. He likes baseball and soccer.
He doesn't like math or history.

_____
_____
_____
_____

Go for it!
Geography

Some cities sound like the names of their countries. Match the countries to the cities.

Algeria — b. Algiers   a. Tunis

Belize   b. Algiers

Brazil   c. Taipei

Dominican Republic   d. Brasilia

El Salvador   e. Belmopan

Guatemala   f. Luxembourg

Luxembourg   g. Guatemala City

Mexico   h. Mexico City

Panama   i. San Salvador

Taiwan   j. Santo Domingo

Tunisia   k. Panama

Look at a book of maps. Where is each country? Fill in the chart.

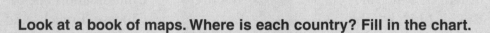

Africa	Asia	Europe	North America	Central America	South America
Algeria					

Unit 14 LESSON A
What are you doing?

1 Number the sentences to make a conversation.

___ No, it's boring. Are you doing homework?

_1_ Hello, Mark.

___ I'm reading a book and listening to a CD.

___ What are you doing?

___ Is the book good?

___ No, I'm not. I'm watching TV.

___ Oh, hello, Sonia.

2 Cross out the word that does not belong.

1. The documentary ~~this~~ program is interesting.
2. They're are reading their books.
3. Do you want what to go shopping?
4. He's cleaning his listening bedroom.
5. He's is doing his laundry.

3 Unscramble the sentences.

1. watching sister TV your Is ?   Is your sister watching TV?

2. are and Mom dinner Dad making ? _____

3. telephone you on talking Are the ? _____

4. cleaning He's his bedroom . _____

5. watching TV a He's show on game . _____

4 **Match to make sentences.**

1. Ellen and Jack are watching
2. Is Dad making
3. What book are you
4. Bob and Leslie are doing
5. Is your brother talking

a. a snack?
b. laundry.
c. TV
d. on the telephone?
e. reading?

5 **Look at the pictures and answer the questions.**

What is your sister doing?

_____

_____

What is he doing?

_____

_____

What is John doing?

_____

_____

What is he doing?

_____

_____

What are we doing?

_____

_____

What is your brother doing?

_____

_____

6 **Imagine two people you know at home. Write two sentences about what each person is doing right now.**

_____

_____

_____

_____

LESSON B **I'm doing my homework.**

7 Read what Tom and Shelly are doing and fill in the chart with checks ✓.

This is Tom and Shelly. They are brother and sister. They go to Greenwood School. Tom is doing his science homework. Science is his favorite class. He's listening to a CD and having a snack. Shelly is doing her music homework. She is watching a music documentary on TV and eating dinner. She's talking to her friend Agnes on the telephone.

	Tom	Shelly
doing homework	✓	
eating dinner		
having a snack		
listening to a CD		
talking on the telephone		
watching TV		

8 Read the email and circle the things Henry is doing today.

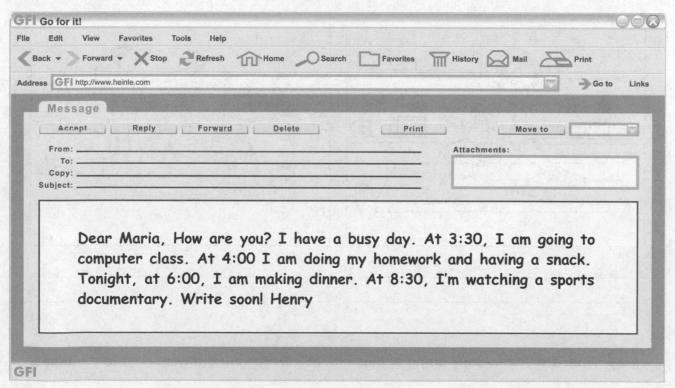

Dear Maria, How are you? I have a busy day. At 3:30, I am going to computer class. At 4:00 I am doing my homework and having a snack. Tonight, at 6:00, I am making dinner. At 8:30, I'm watching a sports documentary. Write soon! Henry

9 Now write an email about what you are doing today.

Dear . . . at . . . o'clock, I am . . .

At school

Where are the students? What are they doing?

_____

_____

_____

_____

10 What are you usually doing at these times? Write your answers next to the times.

1. At 6:00, I am . . . _____

2. At 7:00, I'm . . . _____

3. At 8:00, I am . . . _____

4. At 9:00, I'm . . . _____

5. At 10:00, I am . . . _____

Unit 15
LESSON A
Where's the food court?

1 **Cross out the word that does not belong in each sentence.**

1. Is there a ~~shop~~ sports store near here?
2. Yes, there's is one next to the ATM machine.
3. Is the ATM machine on the two second floor?
4. No, it's on the third floor across from in the food court.
5. Okay. Let's have do lunch at the food court.

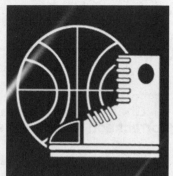

2 **Find these words in the puzzle. Circle the words.**

gym
food
court
video
arcade
movie
theater
sports
store
book
computer
hair
salon
ATM

G	Q	H	E	U	B	Z	A	C	C	H	L	H	A	T
Y	V	I	D	E	O	X	A	R	C	A	D	E	H	M
M	N	C	A	A	E	A	P	E	T	X	S	H	O	P
E	M	X	C	T	T	H	N	G	C	Q	Z	Z	H	T
A	O	W	Q	M	Q	C	H	M	A	E	H	A	A	A
Q	V	S	P	O	R	T	S	X	S	T	O	R	E	A
Q	I	N	Q	Q	L	Q	E	G	H	A	I	R	C	V
H	E	C	Q	A	Q	U	A	F	S	A	L	O	N	T
L	X	Y	H	H	Q	D	P	O	S	O	S	A	M	E
T	T	C	O	M	P	U	T	E	R	T	N	T	H	R
N	H	H	W	Z	A	T	A	L	A	M	E	H	H	H
N	E	N	H	B	O	O	K	T	C	Z	E	H	A	P
Y	A	U	C	H	A	P	N	V	H	T	H	Q	Z	Z
H	T	N	T	F	O	O	D	X	C	O	U	R	T	A
H	E	Q	G	T	Y	H	T	M	H	V	H	A	A	G
N	R	N	H	T	C	Z	E	H	A	P	H	R	T	A

3 (Circle) the correct word.

1. (**Where** / When) is the video arcade?

2. The pet shop is (**across** / in) from the movie theater.

3. The gym is (next to / **between**) the ATM and the sports store.

4. Is there a book store (in / **on**) the second floor?

5. The hair stylist is (**next** / across) to the computer store.

4 Check ✓ the sentences that are correct. Put an ✗ next to the sentences that are not correct and rewrite the sentences.

1. Here are the movie theater.   ✗   Here is the movie theater.

2. Is the gym across from the food court?   ___ _____

3. Is it near from the hair stylist?   ___ _____

4. Is it on the third three floor?   ___ _____

5. The ATM is between the gym not the food court.   ___ _____

5 Unscramble the letters to make words. Then use the words in sentences.

1. texn ot   next to   _____

2. soarcs morf   _____   _____

3. vimeo reettha   _____   _____

4. etp spho   _____   _____

5. teeebwn   _____   _____

6 Number the sentences to make a conversation.

_1_ Hi, Dennis. I'm hungry.

___ It's next to the movie theater.

___ Okay. Let's go eat.

___ The movie theater?

___ There's a food court in the mall.

___ Where is it?

___ Yes. The movie theater is across from the computer store.

Where is it?

LESSON B Is there a park in your neighborhood?

7 Look at the stores and shops and finish the sentences.

1. The supermarket is next to the _____.
2. The bakery is across from the _____.
3. The video store is between the _____ and the _____.
4. The ATM is next to the _____.
5. The ATM is across from the _____.

8 Read about Henry's neighborhood and write the names on the map.

This is my neighborhood. I live in an apartment building with my Mom and Dad and two sisters. Across from our apartment building is a big supermarket. There is a small bakery between the news stand and the supermarket. Across from the bakery is a basketball court. Next to basketball court is a noisy video arcade.

		K			
		i	Henry's apartment		
		n			
		g			
Market Street		S	Market Street		
		t			
		r			
		e			
		e			
		t			

9 What does your neighborhood look like? Draw a map and label the stores and shops. Now, write about your neighborhood.

_____
_____
_____
_____
_____

Cardinal points

Look at the map and use the directions North, South, East and West to fill in the chart.

North	South	East	West
Gym			

Look around. What is North, South, East, and West of you?

_____

_____

_____

Why do you like snakes?

1 Find these words in the puzzle. Circle the words.

quiet	C	Z	R	S	R	J	Q	U	I	E	T	N	M	M	R
intelligent	A	S	I	T	T	F	M	P	R	I	P	M	M	Q	M
cat	T	U	R	T	L	E	P	M	R	Y	A	T	S	I	B
dog	H	T	V	A	M	R	J	G	A	D	R	S	I	R	M
spider	F	F	N	G	Z	R	M	R	T	H	R	P	D	M	I
rat	M	I	F	A	A	E	N	I	B	S	O	I	M	W	T
snake	B	M	M	N	M	T	R	I	A	N	T	D	M	S	R
hamster	N	M	R	J	A	L	Y	N	T	A	T	E	B	B	I
ant	R	S	D	B	D	I	C	T	I	K	M	R	M	M	L
parrot	Y	H	A	M	S	T	E	R	M	E	H	M	R	J	J
ferret	B	M	M	N	M	F	R	I	V	I	H	D	O	G	R
turtle	M	I	N	T	E	L	L	I	G	E	N	T	M	R	J

2 Unscramble the words in each line to make a conversation.

A: see the Let's parrots . <u>Let's see the parrots.</u>

B: like do you Why parrots ? _____

A: intelligent very Because are they . _____

B: they from are Where ? _____

A: from America are They South . _____

3 **Number the sentences to make a conversation.**

____ Intelligent? I think they're scary.

_1_ Let's go to the pet shop.

____ Okay. Let's look at the spiders.

____ Oh, no. They're small and quiet.

____ Oh! Do you like spiders?

____ Yes, I do. They're intelligent.

4 **Cross out the word that does not belong in each sentence.**

1. She doesn't ~~don't~~ like spiders.
2. Why doesn't your mom she like turtles?
3. Because I think thinks they're kind of fun.
4. Why when do you like ferrets?
5. Let's get a two snakes.

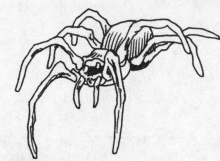

5 **Match the questions and answers.**

1. Why does he like cats.   a. Yes, she does.
2. Does your mom like dogs?   b. Spiders are small.
3. Are ferrets noisy?   c. Because they're intelligent.
4. What's a small pet?   d. No, it's quiet.
5. Is this hamster noisy?   e. No, they aren't.

LESSON B I think dolphins are friendly.

6 Draw a new animal! Add features from three or four different animals. Then, use words from the box to describe your new animal.

silly
interesting
exciting
funny
scary
sad
beautiful
intelligent
fast
shy
friendly
cute

_____

_____

7 Read the paragraph and write the animal names next to its group.

Animals come in groups

Different animals have their own group names. Elephants, for example, come in herds. But the group name **herds** is not used for all animals. Gorillas, for example, come in bands while a group of tigers is a streak. In the air, birds, such as parrots, often come in flocks. Under the water, we say that fish are found in groups called schools.

1. a herd of _____.
2. a flock of _____.
3. a school of _____.
4. a band of _____.
5. a streak of _____.

8 Write about animals you like and animals you don't like. Tell why.

1. I don't like snakes because they're scary. _____
2. _____
3. _____
4. _____
5. _____

Go for it!
Animal habitats

Look at the pictures and write the names of the animals next to the correct habitats. Add other animals you know that live in these places.

panda	dolphin	shark	eagle	gorilla
elephant	tiger	parrot	turtle	

turtle _____

_____

_____

_____

_____

_____

_____

_____

_____

_____

_____

_____

_____

_____

_____

_____

Review 4

1 **Write the missing words in the crossword puzzle.**

Down

2.

4.

5.

6. People in France speak _____.

7.

9. The new baby panda at zoo is very c _____.

11. I'm not happy, I'm _____.

						¹c	o	u	r	²t	
						³		⁴			
⁵		⁶									
			⁷								
⁸								⁹			
				¹⁰							
		¹¹									
¹²											

Across

1. Let's have lunch at the food _____.

3.

7. I don't like thrillers. They're _____.

8.

10. It's not slow, it's _____.

12. That's the new movie _____.

2 (Circle) **the correct word.**

1. What are you ((doing) / talking) after school?

2. I'm (listening / watching) a movie on TV.

3. Let's go to (a / the) food court.

4. No, I watch a movie (every / this) day after school.

5. Okay. I'm (going / on) to the mall with Janice.

3 **Look at the letters in neighborhood. How many other words can you make with these letters?**

hi, do, . . . _____

_____

4 Match the words. Then label the pictures.

1. making
2. computer
3. watching
4. United
5. movie

a. store
b. theater
c. dinner
d. TV
e. Kingdom

5 Fill in the missing letters to spell a new word. Then write sentences using all the words. Try to use more than one word in each sentence.

_____
_____
_____
_____
_____

		_e_	l	e	p	h	a	n	t
	M	e	_	i	c	o			
	l	u	n	_	h				
f	a	s	c	_	n	a	t	i	n	g
		i	n	_	e	l	l	i	g	e	n	t
		t	_	g	e	r			
	l	a	u	_	d	r	y		
d	o	i	n	_					

6 Number the sentences to make a conversation.

____ Hair salon! Don't you take him to a pet shop?

_1_ Hey, Amy. Where are you going?

____ I see. Is there a hair salon near here?

____ I'm taking my dog to the hair salon.

____ Is the hair salon between the food court and the video arcade?

____ Is the food court on the third floor?

____ No, it's on the second floor.

____ Oh, no! He doesn't like the pet shop. It's too noisy.

____ There are two. One is in the mall across from the sports store.

____ Yes. Then I'm taking my dog to the food court for lunch.

Hey, Amy. Where are you going?

My reading journal

Title: Danger on White Water

Author:

I think the story is

What would you take on a rafting trip? Make a list or draw all the things that you need.

Write a dialog of your own.

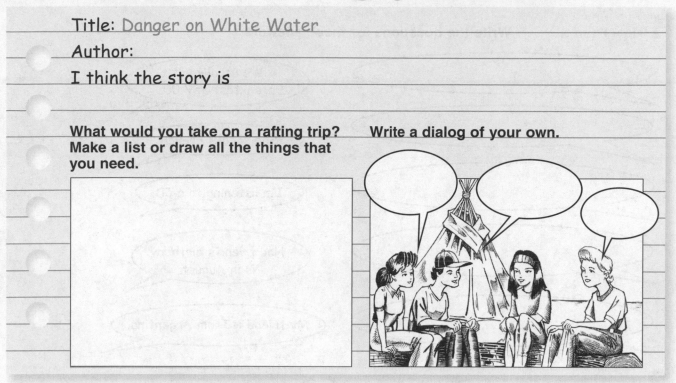

Pretend you are one of the characters in Danger on White Water. **Write an e-mail to a friend. Tell him or her about your trip.**

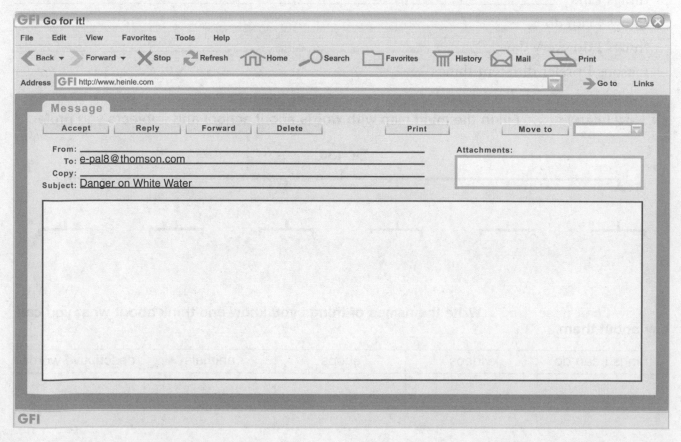

Self check

1 Now I can say . . . **Write the questions for these answers.**

We usually eat breakfast at 7:00.

She speaks French.

I'm listening to a CD.

Her friend's birthday is in August.

My friend is from Argentina.

2 Now I can talk about . . . **Tick the boxes and write an example.**

☐ things I'm doing _____

☐ things I like _____

☐ things I can do _____

☐ things I do every day _____

☐ reasons I prefer different things _____

3 Now I can list . . . **Fill in the mind map with words about school and subjects you prefer.**

School

4 Now I can describe . . . **Write the names of things you know and think about what you can say about them.**

things I can do	videos	shops	animals	descriptive words